Keeping the faith

PRAYERS

 *FOR*

COLLEGE
STUDENTS

KERRY WEBER

**TWENTY-THIRD
PUBLICATIONS**

twentythirdpublications.com

For my family

Eighth printing 2018

TWENTY-THIRD PUBLICATIONS
One Montauk Avenue, Suite 200
New London, CT 06320
(860) 437-3012 or (800) 321-0411
www.twentythirdpublications.com

ISBN 978-1-58595-738-5
Library of Congress Catalog Card Number: 2008943614

Printed in the U.S.A.

A division of Bayard, Inc.

CONTENTS

INTRODUCTION

My flip-flops slapped at the grass as I did my best to sprint across campus in the dark. It was nearly 9 PM, and the cool night air lay still, as if waiting for me to sweep through the quad. Moments earlier I had been seated at my desk in the corner of a cramped room on the 4th floor of McVinney Hall, alternating my gaze from the glaring, empty computer screen to the still unfamiliar walls, as I willed myself not to cry. I spotted the Mass schedule that I had conveniently tacked to the wall, and out of curiosity—or boredom—I read the Mass times. I barely managed to mumble a quick, "I'll be back later," to my roommate, before slipping out the door.

I stumbled into one of the dark wooden pews, just as the priest began his short, solo procession from the sacristy to the altar. I had run toward the chapel to be on time, but I was running from some things, too—the work that had already piled up, the hideous dorm showers, the loneliness that I had felt since my arrival a few weeks earlier.

The chapel was nearly silent. It was not the awkward silence of sharing a room with someone I hardly knew, or the silence of sitting alone at lunch. It was a warm, comforting quiet that felt like home, and I felt no pressure to speak. Here, in the presence of God, I was no longer a nameless freshman, walking in a wandering herd. I bore no label. I was still scared, unsure, and looking for the place where I fit in; but I was no longer alone. God knew me, knew why I was there, and felt no need to make small talk about my major, or my hometown.

I began to go to daily Mass whenever I could make the time. I made a habit of talking to God no matter where I was, or how I felt—grateful, angry, excited, lonely—and I gained strength from our prayerful friendship.

One year later, I hurried toward the chapel for what felt like the millionth time. The construction of a new, larger chapel had been completed since my freshman year, and I could see the steeple from across the quad. I had made a hasty exit after my Habitat for Humanity meeting, and as I walked I checked my watch. I would make it. I slid into a pew beside a group of my friends. After Mass we would probably head to the student center where, over a cup of hot chocolate and a bag of gummi worms, we could discuss anything from my Shakespeare class, to the adventures of being a resident assistant, to my preparations to study abroad. But now, we sat together in the familiar silence.

In the months since my desperate sprint to Mass, it had become obvious that the comfort I felt there extended beyond the walls of the chapel. It was available in all places, at any time, whenever I turned to God in quiet prayer. This book is a starting point, because sometimes, the hardest part is simply finding the words to begin. A dialogue with God does not need to take on a specific form, and we do not need to be intimidated by the idea. God shares our desire for this intimate conversation in prayer, too, and welcomes us whether we rush in desperation toward Christ's comfort, or simply sit quietly, letting the peace of Christ wash over us, like a still night air anticipating our arrival.

COLLEGE LIFE

Beginning the school year

Christ, you, above all, know the significance of new beginnings. Guide me, Lord, that I might take full advantage of this fresh start, always seeking ways to better myself, to make good use of my time, to balance my schoolwork and my extra-curricular activities. May this school year bring new friends, as well as happy reunions with the old. Help me to go forth with faith, and to approach all things with an adventurous spirit, a ready heart, and a willingness to follow where you lead.

All beginnings are somewhat strange; but we must have patience, and, little by little, we shall find things, which at first were obscure, becoming clear. ◆ ST. VINCENT DE PAUL

First time sharing a room

Lord, I am used to having my own space and dealing only with my own schedule. Help me to adjust, and to learn to take into account another person's schedule, habits, belongings. Help me to see this situation as an opportunity to grow in my capacity for compassion, understanding, patience, and tolerance. It takes time, Lord, to grow used to this new, shared space. Be with us Lord, as we eat, as we sleep, as we wake, as we work, that we might be considerate and respectful of each other at all times. Bless us, Lord, and bless this room, our new home.

Be not anxious about what you have, but about what you are.
♦ POPE ST. GREGORY

Difficult roommate

We come from different homes and different backgrounds. We have different interests, and separate groups of friends. If it were not for this space we share, it seems (Name) and I would have nothing in common. Help me Lord, to have patience as (Name) and I adjust to this new living situation. Though we may not always agree, help us to treat each other with courtesy and respect. Grant us the patience to listen, to learn, and to heal our relationship, that we might live together peacefully. Help me always to acknowledge your presence here with us, and to see that despite our differences, we are united in your name and by your love.

We can never love our neighbor too much.
♦ ST. FRANCIS DE SALES

Choosing a major

Sometimes this seems an impossible choice. Guide me as I discern your will for my life. Help me to choose a field in which I will thrive, and to choose a major based not on its convenience or popularity, but because it is a subject I love. Guide my choice, Lord, and throughout my course of study, guide me toward my vocation. Form my mind, that I can make best use of the gifts and talents you have given me. With a passionate heart, a willing mind, and your love, always with me, I cannot go wrong.

The real tragedy in life is not in being limited to one talent, but in the failure to use the one talent. ◆ EDGAR W. WORK

Academic pressures

So much is expected of me, Lord. I feel constant pressure to succeed, to improve. Be with me when my classes overwhelm me, when I am afraid of failure, when I worry about disappointing my professors, my parents, and myself. Lord, calm my mind and help me to see that you truly know and appreciate the effort and diligence I put into my work. May I use my knowledge and abilities to glorify you. May I always recognize the pleasure in simply learning something new, whether from my books or my mistakes. Guide me as I study, as I read, as I learn so that my work, my efforts, are done in your name and for you alone.

If you're always striving to find some new way to grow, to improve, to better your skills and talents, you'll always be successful, both in the eyes of others and in your own eyes.
◆ CYNTHIA KERSEY

Getting an on-campus job

Lord, thank you for the opportunity presented by
this new job. May I appreciate this chance to take
on responsibility, and to earn money so that I can
contribute to my tuition or rent, put gas in my car, or
simply buy a pizza (or list your personal reasons for
gratitude). Though sometimes I feel as though the last
thing I need is more work, help me to see the value in
the companionship of my coworkers, the benefits of
experience, and the chance to serve others through my
work.

Work spares us from three evils: boredom, vice, and need.
◆ VOLTAIRE

Learning new, regional terminology

Help me to understand, Lord, when it seems as though
my friends are speaking another language. Whether
we're eating "grinders," "heroes," or "hoagies";
sharing a "pizza" or a "pie"; or sipping "soda" or "pop"
on a "wicked" hot day, help me to appreciate these
differences, if only for their comedic value, while always
advocating for the universal adoption of my hometown
vocabulary.

*Slang is a language that rolls up its sleeves, spits on its hands
and goes to work.*
◆ CARL SANDBURG

Writing a paper

Holy Spirit, inspire me. When I am overwhelmed by the emptiness of my computer screen, a lack of ideas, or a temptation to give up, focus my thoughts, and keep my mind free from distraction. Guide me so that what I write may be thoughtful, deliberate, and uniquely my own. Give me the courage to be creative, confidence in my ability, and the determination needed to complete my work on time.

The secret of getting ahead is getting started. The secret of getting started is breaking your complex, overwhelming tasks into small manageable tasks, and then starting on the first one.
◆ MARK TWAIN

An all-nighter

In the quiet hours of the evening, the still hours in the middle of the night, and in the early morning, help me to focus on my work, to do my best, and to remain calm. Help me, Lord, to maintain my concentration, but inspire me to also recognize the importance of rest. Give me strength when I am weary, Lord, and provide me with the energy—and coffee—to get through tomorrow.

Never say to God, "Enough"; simply say, "I am ready."
◆ BLESSED SEBASTIAN VALFRE

Making a college sports team

Lord, thank you for giving me the strength, the
perseverance, the will to succeed. Help me to become
stronger in mind and body, as I seek to improve my
skills. Guide me, Lord, that through the talents you have
given me, I might better this team and myself, and grow
in my relationship with you.

*I learned that if you want to make it bad enough, no matter
how bad it is, you can make it.* ◆ GALE SAYERS

Becoming a member of a club

It is a blessing, Lord, to contribute to something larger
than myself. Guide me that I might offer this group my
own unique talents. Unite our community of members
in our common interest and goal, and help us to share
fully in each other's gifts. Guide us, Lord, that our group
might reflect the unity of all your people, and always
welcome all those whom we meet.

*To be needed in other human lives—is there anything greater
or more beautiful in this world?* ◆ HONORÉ DE BALZAC

Service

You call us to serve, Lord,
    to open ourselves to others.
Sometimes I get discouraged because it seems impossible

for me to make a difference,
But when I look into the eyes of a woman in prison,
    when I serve a meal to the hungry,
    build houses for the homeless,
    when I see all that is left to do,
I know that it is impossible not to try.
I cannot do everything,
    but all that I can accomplish,
    I do through you.
Give me the courage to continue your work on earth.
As my eyes are opened to the suffering in this world,
    help me to act on this knowledge,
    and to see it not as a burden,
but as a blessing that draws me closer to you.

*The bread that you store up belongs to the hungry; the cloak
that lies in your chest belongs to the naked; the gold that you
have hidden in the ground belongs to the poor.*

        ◆ ST. BASIL THE GREAT

Those elected to student government

Lord, help me to be true to the mission of this college,
    my fellow students, myself,
    and most importantly, to you.
Help me to represent those who have placed
    their trust in me.
Guide me so that I might make decisions responsibly,
    listen respectfully to the views of others,

and lead with gentleness and dignity.
Lord, may I always remember that my strength,
    my power comes from you,
Thank you for the privilege of serving my fellow students,
    the college, and the community, in your name.

*The moment we understand that we are no more than
instrumentens of God is a beautiful one.*
◆ ARCHBISHOP OSCAR ROMERO

....

An athlete's prayer

For strength and skills, I thank you, Lord.
Inspire me,
that I might have diligence in my training,
that I might use my athletic gifts to the best of my ability,
that I might strive to improve myself
    as both an athlete and a person.
At times, balancing my training with my schoolwork
    can be difficult,
but help me to remember that it is important
    to strengthen my body, mind, and spirit.
Guide me so that these aspects of myself
    may always work in harmony,
as a form of prayer and praise for your creation.
Help me always to respect my teammates,
    my coaches, my competitors, and my own body.
Instill in me a healthy spirit of competition
    and a balanced perspective,

grounded in the awareness that you, above all,
   are my strength.

I have competed well; I have finished the race; I have kept the faith.
                                                    ◆ 2 TIMOTHY 4:7

....

A resident assistant's prayer

Lord, give me the strength
   to face the challenges of my job,
   to set a good example,
   to act with kindness and understanding
   toward the students around me.
When my fellow students turn to me, let me turn to you.
Help me to offer to them what you give to all of us:
   a true community,
   guidance in a time of uncertainty,
   hope in times of sadness,
   trust, safety, respect, comfort,
   an open door.
Help me to listen truly,
   and to trust that when I am in need of an answer,
   a question, inspiration, a plan, courage,
   you will provide.
I am not here to judge, but to be fair and loving,
   to help others to know that they are not alone.
Help me to know that I am not alone,
   and that my work is your work,
and it is worth continuing.

The Christian ideal has not been tried and found wanting. It has been found difficult and left untried.

◆ G.K. CHESTERTON

Intramural league athlete

Lord, thank you for this opportunity to come together as both teammates and friends. Help our team to play at our best, to engage in a friendly spirit of competition, and to hopefully, one day, become the proud owners of an intramural league champion T-shirt. Amen.

The way a team plays as a whole determines its success. You may have the greatest bunch of individual stars in the world, but if they don't play together, the club won't be worth a dime.

◆ BABE RUTH

Having a class outside

Lord, thank you for the opportunity to learn in the midst of your beautiful creation: the warm weather, the professor redoubling efforts to get the class to pay attention, the student avoiding the bugs, another picking at the grass. Let this time outside remind me of the importance of stepping outside my own thoughts, and of being an active part of the body of Christ. Help me to see the ways in which I can apply what I learn in class to my life, to the world. As I enjoy the warmth of the sun, the bright blue blanket of sky, the birds, the grass, the breeze, let me always remember that learning extends far beyond the walls of the classroom, and there is so much left to explore.

The trees and the stones will teach you what you will never learn from the masters. ◆ ST. BERNARD OF CLAIRVAUX

Prayer for my professors

Bless my professors, Lord, that their enthusiasm for their subject will be conveyed in their lectures, and inspire a sense of curiosity in me. May their words encourage us, as students, always to seek knowledge and truth. Grant them patience in their classes that they might foster valuable discussion, and may each of us keep an open mind that we might always learn from each other.

The wisest mind has something yet to learn.
◆ GEORGE SANTAYANA

Having the opportunity to take courses that reflect a desired career

Lord, it is amazing to me sometimes that my classes do not feel at all like work. It is an incredible blessing to have the opportunity to learn about a subject in which I am genuinely interested, to focus on school, on bettering myself, on preparing myself for my career, my goals.

Lord, help me to be attentive so that the knowledge I obtain might inspire me to continue to seek truth and to strive, always, to better myself and the world.

Far away there in the sunshine are my highest aspirations. I may not reach them, but I can look up and see their beauty, believe in them, and try to follow where they lead.

◆ LOUISA MAY ALCOTT

A stimulating class or conversation

Lord, thank you for the opportunity to discuss and debate so many topics with my fellow students and my professors. I am grateful for the chance to share my ideas and to listen to those around me, though we may not always agree. Lord, give me the courage to participate and to speak my mind, even if I must stand on my own. May I always be open to the abundance of knowledge and ideas that surround me, and allow myself to grow, share, and listen throughout these passionate discussions.

A single conversation across the table with a wise person is worth a month's study of books. ◆ CHINESE PROVERB

Study abroad

Lord, bless my journey. Help me to enter this new country, this new culture, gently and with respect. May I be open to the new experiences, customs, and people that I will encounter—whether I am asking for directions in Spanish, navigating my way through busy streets on a bicycle, or politely sampling haggis. Inspire my thoughts, my work, my travels. Bless me, Lord, so that I might return with new insights and see my own home with new eyes.

The whole object of travel is not to set foot on foreign land; it is at last to set foot on one's own country as a foreign land.
♦ G.K. CHESTERTON

. . . .

Exam period

Lord, during these stressful days it seems impossible to process all that I have learned. Stay with me, Lord, as I prepare for my exams. When I am overwhelmed, help me maintain a balanced perspective, to see the value in taking breaks. May I always view learning as a lifelong process, comprised only in part by these exams. Help me to remember that you are beside me in every exam, every test, every trial life may provide.

Without work, it is impossible to have fun.
♦ ST. THOMAS AQUINAS

. . . .

Prayer right before an exam

Lord, calm my nerves and focus my thoughts that I might remember, comprehend, and relate, to the best of my abilities, all that I have learned about the subject at hand.

Believe in yourself! Have faith in your abilities! Without a humble but reasonable confidence in your own powers you cannot be successful or happy. ◆ NORMAN VINCENT PEALE

Prayer before school break

Lord, it is such a relief to take a break from the busy schedule of the school year. Help me to use this time to refocus, relax, and to enjoy the company of friends or family members. Guide me, Lord, whether I'm lying on the beach, reading a book, or backpacking through a foreign city. It can be all too easy to lose myself in my work, my studies, the stress of everyday life. Help me to take this time to reconnect with you, my ever-present source of energy, refreshment, and hope.

It is such a folly to pass one's time fretting, instead of resting quietly on the heart of Jesus. ◆ ST. THÉRÈSE OF LISIEUX

Ending the school year

Christ, you, above all, know that those things that seem like endings are quite often new beginnings. This school has come to feel like home, and it seems strange to leave my friends and this campus for the summer. I will miss this place, but I will take with me so many memorable experiences and friendships from this past year. Lord, open my eyes to the unique opportunities and freedoms offered in the coming months. Help me to continue to grow, to work, to rest, so that I will return in the fall, refreshed, ready, and with a renewed vision, prepared to begin the next part of this great adventure.

The beginning and the end reach out their hands to each other.
◆ CHINESE PROVERB

. . . .

Graduation

As the school year draws to a close, I know I'm ready to leave, to move on, but I also know that there are so many parts of college life that I will miss. Over the past few years I have more fully become the person I am meant to be, but I know that I have a great deal left to learn. Help me to see that though this place has become a part of me, it does not define me; there is so much that lies ahead. Give me the courage to face the uncertain future and to accept and appreciate myself just as I am right now, at once wondering, worrying, and searching. Help me to cherish this moment, and each moment as everyday life comes at me, carrying with it many answers and an infinite number of questions. I don't know exactly how this next step in my life will unfold, or how it will feel to leave this place that has become my home. Give me your strength, Lord. I know that to be prepared, I need only you.

There is a great deal of unmapped country within us.
◆ GEORGE ELIOT

GRATITUDE

A good roommate

Lord, I am so grateful for the opportunity to share a room with (Name). It is a blessing to live with someone who understands me, and with whom I can share my thoughts, my food, and if need be, my wardrobe. May we always see your presence in our times together—in our laughter, our friendship, our home.

> *Perhaps the most delightful friendships are those in which there is much agreement, much disputation, and yet more personal liking.* ◆ GEORGE ELIOT

Meeting interesting people

Thank you, Lord, for the opportunity to meet so many people who possess a variety of interests, talents, hobbies, and styles. Help me to see how much there is to learn from those around me: the friend who can juggle, the guy from Bulgaria, the girl who speaks four languages (insert your own intentions). May the variety of backgrounds, interests, and beliefs held by those around me serve to make me more aware of the value of diversity, and more mindful of my own views, my own talents, my own unique gifts.

*Be who you are and say what you feel, because those who mind
don't matter and those who matter don't mind.* ◆ DR. SEUSS

. . . .

A friendly smile from a passerby

Thank you, Lord, for the unexpected kindness of a
stranger. Let their smile serve as a reminder that we are
all connected, we all belong, and we all deserve respect.
Bless him/her, Lord, with your kindness, as they have
blessed me.

Kindness is the golden chain by which society is bound together.
◆ JOHANN WOLFGANG VON GOETHE

. . . .

A good grade

Lord, may this accomplishment inspire me to continue
to do my best work. It is gratifying to know that my
time, effort, and hard work have been acknowledged.
Help me to remember that the benefits of persistence
and a good work ethic reach far beyond the classroom.
Continue to guide me, Lord, in my efforts to better
myself and my work in your name, for you are the
ultimate judge of all my thoughts, my words, of all that
I do.

Energy and persistence conquer all things.
◆ BENJAMIN FRANKLIN

An accomplished and completed project

Thank you for guiding me in my work, Lord. Thank you for the process, which has given me the chance to learn about this subject and about myself—whether that means recognizing the need to start my work earlier, that I am a perfectionist, or that I harbor an extreme dislike of calculus. Help me simply to be grateful that I have finished, and for the chance to finally—and if only for a moment—relax.

By perseverance the snail reached the ark.

◆ CHARLES H. SPURGEON

Someone folded my laundry

For once, Lord, my clean laundry has stayed that way. Thank you for keeping it from being dumped into a sopping heap on a dryer or thrown, warm and dry, onto a dusty table. To have my clothes folded, my socks matched, and everything in order and smelling of fabric softener, seems, at times, like a little bit of heaven on Earth.

We should all do what, in the long run, gives us joy, even if it is only picking grapes or sorting laundry. ◆ E.B. WHITE

Admiring a huge academic library

Lord, I am always in awe of the amount of knowledge contained in this place. Each book holds a piece of information that is within my reach. Each page represents a new possibility, new ideas, the unlimited potential of the human mind. I cannot learn everything, Lord, but when I'm in here, I think it might be fun to try. Inspire me, Lord, that I might always appreciate the opportunity offered to me in this place of learning.

The reading of good books is like a conversation with the best [people] of past centuries—in fact like a prepared conversation, in which they reveal only the best of their thoughts.
◆ RENÉ DESCARTES

A nod of approval from a professor

Lord, when I am poring over my books in the library or holed up in the computer lab, it is easy to feel that my efforts are going unnoticed. Thank you, Lord, for the kind words of a professor that serve as a small reminder that I am improving, learning, growing, changing. Though I know the approval of others is not the aim of my work, kind words are encouraging, and I am so grateful to hear that I am doing well.

Kind words do not cost much, yet they accomplish much.
◆ BLAISE PASCAL

Understanding

Thank you, Lord, for the gift of understanding. The

distance between myself and a calculus problem or a Shakespearean sonnet, seems, at times, insurmountable. It is such a relief and a blessing to finally comprehend this seemingly impossible topic. Thank you for giving me the strength to persevere. Though I know there are some things in life that may never quite make sense, it is nice to know that there is so much that is worth knowing and that the learning process itself can be its own reward.

Learn everything you possibly can, and you will discover later that none of it was superfluous. ◆ HUGH OF SAINT-VICTOR

. . . .

Church community at school

Lord, thank you for the gift of this faith community. May we as individuals always be willing to lend support, encouragement, and kindness to each other and, in this way, strengthen our friendship, our faith, and your kingdom here on Earth.

The Church is not made up of people who are better than the rest, but of people who want to become better than they are.

◆ ANONYMOUS

. . . .

Support of friends, family, professors

Lord, thank you for the support offered by (Name). It is a comfort to know that I am not alone. As I grow, learn, and travel, I know that their kindness is always with me, and lends me courage to continue to strive to do your will.

I am part of all that I have met. ♦ ALFRED TENNYSON

. . . .

Finding a quiet place

Thank you for this moment of rest, Lord,
   amidst the shuffle, the struggle,
   the rushing of everyday life.
As I sit and listen—beneath a tree,
   in a corner of the library, in my room—
may I feel your presence, speak to you,
   and know that you, too, are listening.

Not all of us are called to be hermits, but all of us need enough silence and solitude in our lives to enable the deeper voice of our own self to be heard at least occasionally.
♦ THOMAS MERTON

. . . .

At sunrise

As the sun brings with it a new morning, so do you provide me with a fresh start, Lord. As I begin my day, enlighten my mind, warm my heart, and energize my spirit with your light, your love, your hope.

What is the good of your stars and trees, your sunrise and the wind, if they do not enter into our daily lives? ♦ E.M. FORSTER

At sunset

Give me peace, Lord, at the day's end. As the sun sets
and night arrives, let these brilliant, fleeting colors serve
as a reminder to appreciate each moment of life, never
worrying about what is to come, knowing that you will
be with me in darkness and in light.

God is closer to us than water is to a fish.
♦ ST. CATHERINE OF SIENA

A snowy day

Lord, thank you for this clean, white slate of snow that
offers endless possibilities: building snow men on the
quad, a snowball fight, a quiet walk through the still
winter air. Help me always to see your love, your beauty
in a snowfall that arrives softly, quietly in the winter
night. I know that come morning, the whole world will
be transformed.

*In the depths of winter I finally learned there was in me an
invincible summer.* ♦ ALBERT CAMUS

A rainy day

Thank you, Lord, for the refreshment this rain
provides. Help me to see the weather not as an
inconvenience, but as part of the beautiful variety
of life. May I always remember that it is up to me to

decide whether I rush through the rain in life, hoping to escape unscathed, or to walk calmly, soaking in all that surrounds me.

There is no such thing as bad weather. All weather is good because it is God's. ◆ ST. TERESA OF AVILA

. . . .

A wonderful day

It is days like this, Lord, when everything seems to come together, that I feel so grateful just to be alive. Whether my joy comes from an exciting class, a cancelled class, chicken nuggets in the cafeteria, a good grade, beautiful weather, Frisbee on the quad, or time spent laughing with friends, all of it reminds me of the beauty of this world and the many ways in which I am blessed. Thank you, Lord, for this gift. Help me to feel this wonder, this gratitude, every day of my life.

Yesterday is gone. Tomorrow has not yet come. We have only today. Let us begin. ◆ MOTHER TERESA

. . . .

Beautiful weather

Lord, the beauty of your creation surrounds me every day, but today I am especially aware of the miracles of the sun, the sky, the trees. It seems as though all elements of nature have come together to create a perfect day, and I cannot help but feel I, too, am a part of all of this beauty. Help me always to feel this communion with nature and through its beauty, with you.

My soul can find no staircase to heaven unless it be through Earth's loveliness. ◆ MICHELANGELO

....

Prayer of gratitude

At times, I am simply awed by the blessings in my life. I am so grateful to you, the origin of all that is good in this life. Today, I am particularly grateful for (intention). May I always respect and appreciate the gifts and talents you have given me. Keep me from taking my family and friends for granted. Inspire me to express my gratitude more often, that I might always be reminded of the blessings in my life, of your constant, unfailing love.

In ordinary life we hardly realize that we receive a great deal more than we give, and that it is only with gratitude that life becomes rich. It is very easy to overestimate the importance of our own achievements in comparison with what we owe others. ◆ DIETRICH BONHOEFFER

FRIENDS & FAMILY

Making friends

The continuous effort of making connections and beginning new friendships can be exhausting. Give me patience, Lord, with myself and with those whom I meet. Keep me from judging too quickly, or fearing what others think of me. Help me to value this journey we share at this unique time in our lives and to see the infinite possibilities for joy in these new relationships. Help me to see that you are always with me, my constant friend, as I begin this new part of my life. Give me the wisdom to see that these new friends do not need to replace the old, but can help me to grow in love and in my friendship with you.

At the corner of Fourth and Walnut, in the center of the shopping district, I was suddenly overwhelmed with the realization that I loved all those people...that we could not be alien to one another even though we were total strangers.

◆ THOMAS MERTON

Keeping ties with old friends

Lord, I am incredibly grateful for my long-time friends. They have helped to form the person I have become and have changed my life in so many ways. As I continue to grow, learn, and explore, help me to remain close to these friends, and to rejoice in their friendship. As we meet new people, travel to different places, and encounter new experiences, our paths in life may not always be the same. I pray that despite distance we may remain close, and always value the time we have spent together. May we look forward to the future knowing that all friends united by your love are never far apart.

To know someone here or there with whom you feel
there is understanding in spite of distances or thoughts
unexpressed—that can make of this earth a garden.
◆ JOHANN WOLFGANG VON GOETHE

Newfound friend

Thank you, Lord, for the gift of this person who brings out a new part of me, who will become a part of my life, and my college experience. I am blessed to find another person who understands me, who shares my interests or my sense of humor. Nourish our friendship, that our time together may be filled with kindness, loyalty, and laughter.

Faithful friends are beyond price: No amount can balance
their worth.
◆ SIRACH 6:15

A special moment or inside joke

Lord, thank you for sending me someone who understands me: my sense of humor, my tastes. Thank you for the gift of this person who knows me so well they understand what I am saying while I am brushing my teeth; someone who knows that when I wear a certain sweatshirt, I'm having a bad day; someone who agrees to drive me around when it snows, because they know it stresses me out, or knows when I just need to be left alone (insert your own examples). May these moments of true friendship always serve to bring us closer together and help us to see your presence in our shared laughter, our mutual understanding.

There is nothing on this earth more to be prized than true friendship. ◆ ST. THOMAS AQUINAS

. . . .

An unexpected phone call or visit from a high school friend

I feel so blessed to have heard from (Name) today. Amidst all that goes on at school, all the changes of my life here, his/her call/visit provides a sense of comfort, continuity, and familiarity, and a chance to connect the old and the new. Thank you, Lord, for this opportunity to be refreshed by this conversation, this friendship, the shared memories that serve as a reminder of your presence in all things, a reminder of home.

It is one of the blessings of old friends that you can afford to be stupid with them. ◆ RALPH WALDO EMERSON

An unexpected care package or card

Lord, there's nothing like real mail. It's a great feeling to be remembered and to have something tangible in a familiar handwriting, from someone I love. I welcome whatever is sent to me: the note, the snacks, the clean socks. Help me to be open to you in the same way, Lord. May I always see these gifts as reminders of your unfailing ability to provide exactly what I need, even when I least expect it.

A friendship can weather most things and thrive in thin soil; but it needs a little mulch of letters and phone calls and small, silly presents every so often—just to save it from drying out completely.   ◆ PAM BROWN

A fellow student in tough times

Lord, your beloved friend John knew the hurt of watching you suffer. I too, must stand by while my friend is in pain, and it seems that there is little I can do to ease his/her burden. I do not know exactly how my friend feels, but I do know what it is like to be confused, sad, troubled, hurt. Give me the strength to lend support in any way I can. Help me to listen attentively and to act with patience and compassion. Help (Name) to find comfort in our friendship and to know that you too are his/her friend, and always present.

It is tough to watch those we love in pain. But we must believe

that by being strong and supportive we make an enormous difference. ◆ JOSEPH CARDINAL BERNARDIN

....

A romantic relationship

Thank you for the gift of this loving relationship. I feel so incredibly blessed to have (Name) in my life right now. I pray that our friendship and love continue to thrive while we are together: in our long talks, the comfortable silences, our inside jokes, our shared sorrows. Help us to appreciate the unique gifts we each bring to the relationship. When we disagree, help us truly to listen to each other and to speak only with patience and kindness. May our relationship always bring with it new and exciting opportunities and ever increasing joy. Let us live so that our friendship and love may always encourage our growth as individuals and as a couple. Guide us, Lord, on our shared path, that we might always move closer to you.

Love is essential, so that without love all our efforts are in vain, no matter how much good we accomplish.
◆ ST. ANTHONY OF PADUA

....

Going out on a first date

I don't know where this will lead, Lord, but I'm excited about the possibilities. Right now, I feel a great sense of hope, combined with a bit of nerves. Help me, Lord, to keep my mind free from worry, my teeth free from food, and help me to find, in this new relationship, a friendship that will lead me closer to you.

There is no instinct like that of the heart.   ◆ LORD BYRON

. . . .

A road trip with friends

Keep us safe, Lord, as the highways stretch out before us. Protect us as we drive, as we eat, as we sleep, as we rest. Help us to meet all that lies ahead with an open heart, to see every turn, every stop, as an adventure. Help us to be patient while in traffic, calm if we get lost, and to always have a good supply of songs for the journey. Be with us Lord, as we explore the road ahead.

The world is a book, and those who do not travel read only a page.   ◆ ST. AUGUSTINE

. . . .

Finding a new and exciting hangout to share with your friends

Lord, you know the importance of community among friends, of having a place to meet, and to enjoy each other's company. We are united in friendship, in our interests, but it is comforting to have a tangible place—a park, a restaurant, a dorm, a pub—that unites us as a group of friends. Help us always to know that you, too, are present in this place and in any place in which we are gathered.

Every now and then go away, have a little relaxation. For when you come back to your work, your judgment will be surer.

◆ LEONARDO DA VINCI

. . . .

Heading home for the first time

Lord, thank you for the opportunity to return home, to see the familiar buildings, my own bedroom, to shower without wearing shoes. Give me the grace to share the changes in my life, in my thoughts and feelings, with my family. Help them to understand that I have grown and changed, but I am still myself. It is not always easy to return to a place that is at once familiar and foreign. Help me to gain strength through this time at home, and to grow closer to my family. May I use this time at home to rest, to remember, and to return to school refreshed.

Home interprets heaven. Home is heaven for beginners.

◆ CHARLES H. PARKHURST

. . . .

Spending time with friends late at night

Thank you, Lord, for late nights and greasy food.
Thank you for this unique time
   —these hours filled with excitement,
   laughter, exhaustion—
that turn a simple conversation into a heart to heart,
   and foster the type of crazy ideas
   that turn into campus legends.

Let these late hours with friends serve as a reminder
that life, when lived properly, is never boring.

Of course life is bizarre, the more bizarre it gets, the more
interesting it is. The only way to approach it is to make yourself
some popcorn and enjoy the show.   ◆ DAVID GERROLD

....

Those at the school who make everything possible

At times I become so overwhelmed I forget those
who make so many parts of my college life possible.
Bless those who serve this college, Lord: For the
cafeteria workers who prepare and serve my food,
for the resident assistants who provide support,
for the security guards who keep our campus safe,
for the janitorial staff who maintain cleanliness,
for the librarians who catalogue our books, for the
administrators who better the school, for student
leaders who plan events on campus, and for the
professors who prepare our exams and lessons and pass
on their knowledge to eager minds. Lord, bless all those
who, in any capacity, serve this school, its students, and
you through their good works, their kindness, and their
presence here on campus.

One must not always think so much about what one should
do, but rather what one should be. Our works do not ennoble
us; but we must ennoble our works.   ◆ MEISTER ECKHART

TIMES OF TROUBLE

. . . .

When feeling homesick

Lord, I am completely overwhelmed,
   and everything around me
   seems foreign.
I feel so far from the comfort
   of my old friends,
   my family,
   my home.
As days pass and new faces and buildings
   become more familiar,
help me to see the potential for a new home
   here at school.
Give me the courage to reach out to others,
   and the willingness to make the effort needed
   to find my place here.
Open my eyes to the unique sources of comfort,
   friendship, opportunity, and growth
   that surround me.
May I never forget that you are always with me,
   no matter where I am;
and wherever you are, I am home.

The value of life does not depend upon the place we occupy. It depends upon the way we occupy that place.

◆ ST. THÉRÈSE OF LISIEUX

Loneliness

Lord, at times it feels like I am the only person who has not yet found a group of friends, a seat at lunch, or made plans for the weekend. I sometimes feel as though I am invisible to everyone around me. Help me to see that there is a place for me here if I am willing to look for it. Give me the courage and persistence to seek out new friendships, and help me to recognize when others reach out to me. Help me to recognize that this college is an ever-changing community, constantly incorporating people of many interests, backgrounds, and beliefs. When I feel isolated or lonely, Lord, give me the strength to continue, knowing that you are with me, and I am never truly alone.

Jesus did not come to explain suffering, but to fill it with his presence. ◆ PAUL CLAUDEL

Crisis in faith

This is not easy,
   talking to you.
I want to believe,
But when I stand in your fields,
   I cannot find peace.
I walk beside the waters, and feel alone.
The world seems dark, and I am afraid.
Help me to empty myself of my fears,
   my pride, my doubts.
Fill me; help me to see your goodness, your kindness.

My Lord, my Shepherd, I am lost.
Find me; guide me home to you.

Faith is not a thing one "loses," we merely cease to shape our lives by it. ◆ GEORGE BERNANOS

Substance abuse/addiction

At times it seems so much easier
   to give myself over to alcohol or to drugs.
They ask nothing of me,
They mask who I am, how I feel, what I think.
But what I want is to be known, to be loved.
I want to depend on you, Lord,
   to feel your love coursing through my veins,
   to drink from your cup.
You ask for so little, only love.
Always, you know who I am, how I feel, what I think.
You lift me higher, Lord.
When all else wears away,
your love remains.

If you do not hope, you will not find what is beyond your hope.
◆ ST. CLEMENT OF ALEXANDRIA

Eating disorder

You multiplied the loaves and the fishes, Lord,
Because you know the importance of nourishment,

both spiritual and physical.
You sent manna to the Israelites wandering in the desert;
    you gave them strength.
Lord, give me the strength to choose nourishment.
I feel as if I am a shadow of my former self.
I want to be whole again.
Help me to see myself as you see me,
    to know that I am beautiful in body and soul.
Your shared meal with your Apostles, Lord,
    was a sign of your love for us.
Help me to find community, support, and love
    when I eat with others.
Help me to be patient with myself,
    to grow, to share in the Paschal feast, and
    to accept your invitation to eat at your table.

A whole bushel of wheat is made up of single grains.

◆ THOMAS FULLER

For a referral to the nearest therapist specializing in eating disorders, contact:

National Association of Anorexia Nervosa and Associated Disorders
P.O. Box 7, Highland Park, IL 60035
1-847-831-3438   http://www.anad.org

National Eating Disorders Association Informational and Referral Program
603 Stewart Street, Suite 803, Seattle, WA 98101
1-800-931-2237   http://www.nationaleatingdisorders.org

When a death in the family occurs while away at school

This time of sadness is so hard for my family and for me.
I long to be closer to my family,
    to offer comfort and to be comforted,
but instead I feel separated and alone.
I am so frustrated by this distance between us,
    by my seeming inability to help.
Lord, help me to see that you can be with my family,
    though I am not.
You hear our prayers.
In our mourning, you give us comfort.
Always, despite this distance, you unite us.

> *Sorrow is a fruit; God does not make it grow on limbs too weak to bear it.*
>   ◆ VICTOR HUGO

Death of a classmate

The seat in class,
The tray at lunch,
The dorm room,
now are empty.
I can't help but feel the same.
I cannot understand it now, Lord.
It seems impossible,
unfair that such a young life could end,
    while still so new,
      so young,

and with so much potential.
I am reminded, painfully, of the frailty
    of my own life as well.
Help me to feel my friend's continued presence and yours,
    here.
Though no longer in class, at lunch, in the dorms,
    my friend remains.
I know that you are always with me,
    and my friend eternally with you.
Embrace us both.

*Our brethren who have been freed from the world by the
summons of the Lord should not be mourned, since we know
they are not lost but sent before.* ◆ ST. CYPRIAN

. . . .

Sexual assault

So much hurt remains, Lord.
I feel so many things:
    fear, anger, pain, vulnerability.
At the same time,
    I feel empty, tired, depleted, numb.
Help me to heal, Lord, to again put my trust in others,
    and in you.
When I am afraid, calm my fears.
When I am angry, teach me to forgive.
Give me the strength to move forward,
    and to see myself as you see me, Lord, with loving eyes.
Though I have been hurt, and my life has changed,

help me to see that I am still beautiful in body and soul,
and I am still loved.

*It is impossible to go through life without trust: that is to be
imprisoned in the worst cell of all, oneself.*

♦ GRAHAM GREENE

The *National Sexual Assault Hotline* can be reached 24 hours a day,
7 days a week at 800-656-4673. When you call, you will hear a
menu and can choose #1 to talk to a counselor. You will then be
connected to a counselor in your area who can help you.

You can also visit the *National Sexual Assault Online Hotline* at
http://online.rainn.org

While struggling with a break-up

This is a difficult time for me, Lord. (Name) has
been a constant in my life, and it is hard to lose his/
her friendship and love. I feel angry, sad, hurt, tired,
anxious, confused. Help me to be grateful for the good
times we spent together, and keep me from dwelling on
my regrets. Though at times it seems as though nothing
will comfort me, keep me pointed toward the future,
toward the possibilities, the friendships that lie ahead.
Help me to use this time to reflect, to grow stronger, to
more fully discover who I have become and what I want
in life. I know this pain will heal, this time will pass. It is
your love, Lord, that makes me whole. Give me strength
to turn to you, to accept your love, your plan for me.

Man has places in his heart which do not yet exist, and into them enters suffering, in order that they may have existence.

◆ LÉON BLOY

Ending self-harm/self-mutilation

There is so much pain inside of me, Lord. Sometimes it feels as though anger, confusion, and sorrow are trapped just beneath my skin. At other times, it seems I cannot feel at all. I create pain to distract from other pains, a pain that fills, only for a moment, that hollow feeling. But this pain does not provide healing. Help me to heal, Lord. Help me to see that hurting myself is not lasting relief, and it is not a cross you want me to bear. You who forgive all things, help me to forgive myself as you do, to see the good you see. Fill me with your love and enable me to see my body as part of your beautiful creation, a life that deserves respect. Give me the courage to seek help and support from others and from you. Guide me that I might fulfill my unique and vital role as a member of your Body in Christ.

God's love for us is not the reason for which we should love God. God's love for us is the reason for us to love ourselves.

◆ SIMONE WEIL

For more information on ending self-harm:

S.A.F.E. Alternatives (Self-Abuse Finally Ends)
www.selfinjury.com   Information Line: 1-800-DONT CUT

While struggling with depression

Lord, it is hard even to begin this prayer.
The extraordinary effort needed to do daily tasks,
    to get out of bed,
    face the world,
    open a book,
    exhausts me.
I feel as though the eyes through which
      I see the world are
    no longer my own.
I am a stranger in my own body,
    weighed down by sadness and apathy.
I long for comfort and relief from this feeling
    inside of me,
but even hope can be exhausting.
Lord, help me to feel your constant presence
    and the presence of those who care for me,
even when I find it hard to care about myself.
Give me the strength and courage
    to seek the help and support I need.
Stretch out your hand to me, Lord;
Reach out and help me to calm this storm.

*All shall be well, and all shall be well, and all manner of
things shall be well.*   ◆ BLESSED JULIAN OF NORWICH

Suicide

At times it feels as though I am never given a chance to catch my breath. I feel pressured, confused, lethargic, frantic, overwhelmed, and numb all at once. I long for relief, for connections, for my life to come together; it sometimes seems impossible. Help me, Lord, to see that I am not alone. My suffering is real, but it can be overcome. Help me to see that my work here on Earth is far from finished. Direct me to where I can be of use, to a place here in this world, where I can feel your presence and feel whole once more.

Where there is life there is hope. ◆ LATIN PROVERB

National Suicide Prevention Lifeline is a 24-hour, toll-free suicide prevention service available to anyone in suicidal crisis. If you need help, please dial 1-800-273-TALK (8255). You will be routed to the closest possible crisis center in your area.

GUIDANCE

Courage to be myself

Lord, the process of self-discovery is long. I sometimes lack the faith to believe that my own opinions, my own abilities are worthwhile. Help me to trust myself, to believe in my own potential, and to express myself more clearly. I want so much to improve myself, to grow in so many ways, but as I struggle with this process, help me to realize the good, the value, that already exists within me. Help me to accept and to love the person I am at this moment, while continuing the journey toward the person I will become. Christ, you were a rebel, and many times you were forced to stand on your own, to speak out for what was unpopular, against what was unjust. Teach me to draw on your strength, to be receptive to your grace. Help me to become more like you and, in the process, more fully the person you call me to be.

Have patience with all things, but first of all with yourself.

◆ ST. FRANCIS DE SALES

Making decisions

Lord, I turn to you for help, that in your wisdom you might aid me in making the right decision. I am unsure about what is best for me, and at times I'm scared to pray for guidance, not because I don't believe, but because I know that if I am honest with myself and with you, I will be changed—and that change scares me. I am comfortable now, and sometimes I am afraid of what you might be calling me to do. Shake me from my comfort. When I doubt my ability to choose what is right, guide me in my discernment and point me in the direction you want me to go. When I turn to you, I will always find the courage to choose faith, the strength to choose hope, the compassion to choose love.

I am not made or unmade by the things which happen to me but by my reaction to them. ◆ ST. JOHN OF THE CROSS

Newfound independence

Lord, this newfound independence is at once exhilarating and exhausting. Each day, from the moment I get out of bed in the morning, until the time I decide to go to sleep, I face decisions and tasks for which I am fully responsible. From laundry, to cooking, to classes, to weekend plans, there is so much that is new, so much to explore, to experience. Help me to move forward without fear. I know that there is so much within me and around me that has yet to be discovered. As I head out on this journey, continually help me to find new energy, new direction in you, knowing that you are by my side, and though I go forward on my own, I am never alone.

*All of us have the power of choice in action at every moment
in our lives.* ◆ ARCHBISHOP FULTON J. SHEEN

. . . .

Protection

Christ, my parent, my friend, my protector
—you are never far from me.
Watch over me as I face the infinite challenges and
experiences of each new day.
Protect me as I work, as I study, as I travel,
as I spend time with friends.
Give me strength to put my trust in you and
to act according to your will.
Your way is not always the easiest, Lord,
and it takes courage to follow where you lead.
Guide my steps, Lord.
Calm my mind.
I know you are by my side through all things,
and I gain strength and comfort
from your protective love.

*Have confidence in your guardian angel. Treat him as a very
dear friend—that's what he is—and he will do a thousand
services for you in the ordinary affairs of each day.*
◆ ST. JOSEMARÍA ESCRIVÁ

. . . .

During times of uncertainty in faith

I long to go back to a time in my life

when I felt more certain—
    More certain about you,
    about my faith,
    my beliefs.
Now, I am not sure what I believe.
As a child, faith comes easily,
    but now it seems that having faith
    requires so much more effort.
I wonder if it is worth it.
Lord, help me to see the value in this search.
Help me to see that faith is not an end,
    but a continuous process
    that I must begin again
    every day.
Only through questioning
    can I find what I truly believe,
    can I strengthen my relationship with you.
I do believe, Lord.
Help my unbelief.

Faith which does not doubt is dead faith.

◆ MIGUEL DE UNAMUNO

To resist peer pressure

You know my thoughts before I speak them,
you know my actions before I do them,
    yet you give me the gift of free will.
You know, also, Lord, how hard it sometimes is

for me to follow you.
I am formed by my freedoms
   —whom I choose as friends,
   how I spend my days and nights.
Sometimes the person they see,
   the person I am with them,
   is not who I want to become,
   who you want me to become.
I want to be liked, Lord, but not at the expense of
   my values,
   my personality,
   my self.
Help me to choose friends who accept me
   as I am.
Give me the courage to be true to myself,
   and most of all to you.

The measure of a person's real character is what he would do if he knew he would never be found out. ◆ THOMAS MACAULAY

....

Balancing everything

I feel like I am running around all day,
   always busy, always moving forward.
My life can be exciting, exhausting, confusing
   —sometimes all these things at once.
It is completely overwhelming at times.
As I move about throughout the day,
   help me never to stray too far from you.

You are with me when I work,
    when I study; at meetings, at parties.
I put my trust in you and know that with your help
    I can handle all things.
Help me to focus on the task at hand
    and never to be afraid or too proud to ask for help.
Help me to see, Lord, the value
    of taking a break,
    of relaxation,
    and of contemplation.
Help me to see that from this stillness springs
    an active, willing, and ready heart.

Don't lose your inner peace for anything whatsoever, even if your whole world seems upset.   ◆ ST. FRANCIS DE SALES

To keep from procrastinating

College life is so busy, Lord, and there are so many
things I want to experience and accomplish. It can be
difficult to prioritize and very easy to convince myself
that there is enough time to do it all. Sometimes simply
thinking about starting a paper, a project, a book, is
overwhelming, and actually completing it can seem
nearly impossible. It can be easier to simply forget about
it, to delay the work, the time, the effort needed to
complete the project. Help me to see that in doing my
work in a timely and thoughtful manner, I am making
the best use of the gifts that you have given to me. Open

my eyes to the joy in work, and in a job well done. Above all, Lord, help me to make you my first priority, because in doing that, all other things will fall into place. May I work each day to gradually build your Kingdom here on earth. Let me begin, again, today.

What good to me was my ability, if I did not use it well?
◆ ST. AUGUSTINE

Discerning a career

Lord, at this point in my life there are so many paths that I can take, and I am unsure of which one is right for me. Walk beside me, Lord, when I feel lost and alone. Guide me toward a career path that is meaningful, and enjoyable. Help me to realize that by choosing a path, I am opening a whole new set of possibilities for my life. Help me to see, Lord, that my opinions are valuable and that I have something unique to offer the world, that I can make a difference in whatever I do. Help me to choose work not for convenience, money, or glory, but let all of my work be your work, my success your success. Guide me toward a path that will lead me not just to my career, but to my calling.

You must be holy in the way that God asks you to be holy. God does not ask you to be a Trappist monk or a hermit. God wills that you sanctify the world and your everyday life.
◆ ST. VINCENT PALLOTTI

Handling Money

Lord, help me to act responsibly when I am dealing with my finances. Whether I am budgeting my monthly costs or paying for my tuition, help me to be mindful of how I spend my money. Give me the wisdom to save appropriately, and the compassion to give generously to those who have less. Keep me from worry, Lord. Never let my thoughts about money distract me from the true wealth of your limitless love.

Nothing that is God's is obtainable by money.

◆ TERTULLIAN

Regarding temptation

Give me strength, Lord, to resist temptations. Help me to reflect on what I have learned from the people I love: my parents, teachers, friends. Then, let me stop for a moment and simply listen to you. Open my heart to your Word, your will, that I might act in accordance with it. Your way is not always the easiest or the most popular, Lord. Help me to recognize when my desires do not coincide with yours. May I always draw strength from your love, and resist those things that separate me from you.

You are not tempted because you are evil; you are tempted because you are human. ◆ ARCHBISHOP FULTON J. SHEEN

Uncertainty

Lord, even as the Israelites wandered for forty years, you never left them, your people. Help me to realize that, as I wander, you are by my side. I am never alone. Though I am uncertain about what I want and in what direction I am heading, may I be patient with myself and know that it is only natural to wonder, to doubt. I long to become more myself, but I am still unsure who I am, or even how to take the first step toward knowing. In this time of questioning, Lord, I want answers. Help me to see you, Lord, as an answer to all things. When I feel empty, fill me with your love. Walk beside me as I discover my purpose here. Christ, my compass, guide me home.

Let nothing trouble you
Let nothing frighten you
Everything passes
God never changes
Patience obtains all
Whoever has God
Wants for nothing
God alone is enough. ◆ ST. TERESA OF AVILA

Maintaining one's values or views while respecting diversity on campus

I need your strength, your patience, Lord. In this environment—through my classes, my books, my fellow students, and my professors—I have been introduced to so many new ideas. I sometimes wonder where my own beliefs fit in. As I listen and learn, give me the courage to examine my beliefs, the strength to maintain my faith, and the knowledge that from this process comes the opportunity to grow closer to you. Help me to see the ways in which I am able to cultivate my own faith through my attentiveness and sensitivity to the opinions and beliefs of others. Help me to go gently into discussions and friendships so that in moments of disagreement, our conversations are not bitter, but blessed in mutual respect. Bless my eyes that I might see as you see. Bless my hands that I may reach out in peace. Bless my lips that I may speak only love.

The point of having an open mind, like having an open mouth, is to close it on something solid. ◆ G.K. CHESTERTON

....

Maintaining honesty and integrity under pressure and during exams

I do not always know the right answer, Lord, in my studies or in my life. In these uncertain times, Lord, calm my mind. Help me to refrain from panic, dishonesty, desperation. Help me to remain focused and thoughtful in my work. Inspire me to produce work that is uniquely my own—created honestly, and with integrity, creativity, and a passion for learning. May I always take pride in my work, while also recognizing how much I have yet to learn.

*While you are proclaiming peace with your lips, be careful to
have it even more fully in your heart.*

◆ ST. FRANCIS OF ASSISI

Prayer before studying, in general

Focus my mind, Lord,
Help me to tune out the distractions of the day,
    to calm my anxieties,
    and to allow myself to be receptive to all
    that I must learn.
It is easy to become discouraged,
    bored, tired, and apathetic,
about studying, preparing for class,
    or completing my work.
Help me to recognize my education as an opportunity to
    improve my mind,
    broaden my horizons,
    and grow in knowledge and wisdom.
Thank you for the privilege of this education.
Help me to see that in studying to the
    best of my ability and learning to my fullest potential,
I more truly participate in life and
I gain a better understanding of myself and your creation.

Why do we educate, unless to prepare for the world?

◆ VENERABLE JOHN HENRY NEWMAN

Guidance for cooperation in a group project

Lord, guide us in our work together. As we strive to reach our shared goal, help us to go gently into this process, to discuss our differences of opinion calmly, and to make best use of our combined knowledge. Help each of us to bring our unique gifts and talents to the group and to contribute to the best of our abilities, so that the finished product is something of which we can all be proud.

One man may hit the mark, another blunder; but heed not these distinctions. Only from the alliance of the one, working with and through the other, are great things born.

◆ ANTOINE DE SAINT-EXUPÉRY

TRADITIONAL PRAYERS

. . . .

Prayer before study by St. Thomas Aquinas

Ineffable Creator...
You are proclaimed
    the true font of light and wisdom,
    and the primal origin
    raised high beyond all things.
Pour forth a ray of your brightness
    into the darkened places of my mind;
    disperse from my soul
    the twofold darkness
    into which I was born:
    sin and ignorance.
You make eloquent the tongues of infants.
    Refine my speech
    and pour forth upon my lips
    the goodness of your blessing.
Grant to me
    keenness of mind,
    capacity to remember,
    skill in learning,
    subtlety to interpret,
    and eloquence in speech.
May you

guide the beginning of my work,
direct its progress,
and bring it to completion.
You Who are true God and true Man,
Who live and reign, world without end. *Amen.*

Our Father

Our Father, who art in heaven,
Hallowed be thy name.
Thy kingdom come;
Thy will be done on Earth as it is in heaven.
Give us this day our daily bread;
And forgive us our trespasses as we forgive those
    who trespass against us;
And lead us not into temptation,
But deliver us from evil. *Amen.*

Hail Mary

Hail Mary, full of grace,
The Lord is with thee;
Blessed art thou among women,
And blessed is the fruit of thy womb, Jesus.
Holy Mary, Mother of God,
Pray for us sinners,
Now and at the hour of our death. *Amen.*

Glory Be

Glory be to the Father, and to the Son,
    and to the Holy Spirit.
As it was in the beginning, is now,
And ever shall be, world without end. *Amen.*

Mealtime Prayer

Bless us, O Lord,
And these your gifts,
Which we are about to receive
From your bounty, through Christ our Lord. *Amen.*

Prayer to Guardian Angel

Angel of God,
My guardian dear,
To whom God's love commits me here;
Ever this day/night be at my side,
To light and guard, to rule and guide. *Amen.*

Apostles Creed

I believe in God, the Father Almighty,
Creator of Heaven and Earth.
I believe in Jesus Christ his only Son, Our Lord.
He was conceived of the Holy Spirit
and born of the Virgin Mary.
He suffered under Pontius Pilate,

Was crucified, died, and was buried.
He descended to the dead.
On the third day, he rose again.
He ascended into heaven and
is seated at the right hand of God,
the Father Almighty.
He will come again to judge the
living and the dead.
I believe in the Holy Spirit,
the Holy Catholic Church,
the Communion of Saints,
the forgiveness of sins,
the resurrection of the body,
and life everlasting. *Amen.*

....

Act of Contrition

My God, I am sorry
for my sins with all my heart.
In choosing to do wrong and
failing to do good,
I have sinned against you
whom I should love above all things.
I firmly intend, with your help,
to do penance,
to sin no more, and
to avoid whatever leads me to sin.
Our Savior Jesus Christ suffered and died for us.
In his name, my God, have mercy. *Amen.*